SPECIES

Species

Published by Bad Betty Press in 2022
www.badbettypress.com

Cover design by Amy Acre
Imagery: Tihiro Ulv/Shutterstock.com

Printed and bound in the United Kingdom

A CIP record of this book is available from the British Library.

ISBN: 978-1-913268-34-3

Supported using public funding by
ARTS COUNCIL ENGLAND

LOTTERY FUNDED

SPECIES

for the ants, and all the sisters

PRESS

The plan is obvious: earth will become more
and more beautiful until I can't stand it.
Then I will vanish.

    – Dennis Nurkse, *A Clearing on Ruth Island*

It doesn't matter if you believe it or not.
The future is coming.

    – Cassandra in *Agamemnon,* Aeschylus

.

Contents

Orphans

The purple sea urchins are not to blame
they have no brain
they graze on kelp, they procreate
until the underwater forest
is a melancholic mess
of spines and mouths
barren, compressed
they cannot stop
they eat and eat and
starve to death.

In Distant Worlds

All my life I waited for you, passionately, bitterly, in silence,
counting the breaths – Dennis Nurkse

In Ithaca, Amy needs a pump installed.
It may only be weeks now, which is to say days.
Mary puts on her shoes and holds her up
for the trip. *Is she scared?* I text Mary,
Is she happy with the life she's had? A question
for the living, I think I know.
What about a body
being reclaimed by the disorder of all things,
the earth recalling her molecules, the sun
revoking her light?
In Ithaca this is happening.
Meanwhile, a world away, you are turning three.
We are reading *Frog and the Birdsong*.
I always forget the dead blackbird.
What is that? you ask.
I tell you, and you say *Why?*

Letter from the Past

We had everything:
water, honey, each other.
Some glaciers were left,
and between the remaining trees
frogs, woodpeckers, even wolves.
You were not yet born.
We were still alive.

Potter's Field, Hart Island Archive

April 14 2020, found poem

Plot 149

Alphonse Bloch, born August 23 1894 in New York, salesman, medical supplies, divorced, died December 6, 1983.

Plot 149

Henry Rosario, guess what Dad, I am so happy Nicole and I went to see you. I hope you like the flowers. [We] will be working very hard to get you out of this place. You deserve better.

Plot 148

June Betts, beloved mother of 3 children, 2 sons, Donald and Stevie, who are in Heaven with her, and 1 daughter, Diane. Sadly, she passed away in a NYC motel room.

Plot 46

My son Gabriele Flores was stillborn. I have no money to bury him.

Plot 175

Female Unknown, Age 25, buried for 33 years.

Plot 145

In June 1983 John Restuccio was found floating in the East River, an apparent suicide. The body was held three weeks waiting for someone to claim it.

Plot 131

Paul Lapidus received his Medical Degree from the University of Odessa. Always interested in Orthopaedic Foot Pathology, [he completed] a Chapter on "The Toenail" shortly before his death.

Plot 131

Haig Krikor Kutukian was born 1896 in Ayntab, Turkey. In 1920 he travelled to the US on the ship La Lorraine, accompanied by his mother and sister. They were ethnic Armenians.

Plot 137

Mr. Ferrick fell into drugs early, went to prison for helping a female companion rob her parents and try to kill them, and died under the wheels of an L train at the Bedford Avenue stop.

Plot 42

Tasha was a good baby! Mommy died just 6 months after Tasha died. Tasha Walker was my baby sister.

Plot 136

William Heitzman was a punk musician who went by the name of Billy Balls. In summer 1982 Billy was shot in his storefront apartment by an unknown person. He lived for 10 days before dying.

Plot 168

Roosevelt Dunn is buried on the eastern shore of Hart Island. His grave can now be re-excavated. No one is buried forever in New York.

Plot 189

Ann Rubin, the mother who never came home.

We Have These Years

a momentary understanding:
the burnt forest will not
return, will not
make its own rain again.
We hold despair at bay,
reckless orphans of destruction.
We have these perfect years,
holding hands at the cafe,
watching people being
busy being people,
indulging sweet distraction,
this forward movement,
still alive.

OK Cupid

You thought it meant something
when you received my ping.
Later you were miffed
that I swiped right on everyone
with hair. (Why pay
for Premium?)

Remember our second date?
Dinner in a yurt, the dinosaur you ate.
I wore a buttoned shirt.
We walked up Uetliberg at night,
I pretended to be fitter than I was,
you hid your erection and your fears.

And on the long walk back,
when I leaned into you and said
my mental health is excellent,
you didn't balk.

Economics

for Walter Scheidel

The extraction rate is the percentage
the powerful take for themselves,
historically trending to the max.
Only catastrophic war or plagues restack
the odds for a while.

The maximum extraction rate
allows others just enough to survive.
It's not kindness but sample bias:
those without the minimum fall out
of the data set, because they died.

On the Other Hand

sometimes
an oak tree
happens

and when it does
it happens
for a long time

Humans

I live in the gut of a roaring truck.
Stillness is the opposite
of what I have been.
Should we move to the country?
you ask. But I long
for a deeper leaving.
I want to be a mushroom
throwing its net into the dark soil,
a bush by the side of a creek
offering my leaves.

Kindred

Babies are not serious people,
judging by the one
I met, who's only interested
in all the ways
the world and life in it
are fun: a rubber band,
a nut, a yellow cargo tram.

Gravity

All through Spring
his words slip away,
carrying life away.
His feet fill slowly
with water, his anger
turns mild.
In the fall, fog falls
on the city every night.
No visits, only video calls.

It's the nature of things
to be heavy. That's what mass does:
yearning for the center of the Earth.
The goggled nurse
holds up his head
with rubber gloves, calls him
though her mask:
Günther, Günther, Günther,
she insists, I think, too much.

Questions

All my life I wanted to be a person.
Is it that we're fifty, you ask
or are things really getting worse?
Can it be both—
the body in its soft decay,
speaking to the earth
stripped of her poison frogs,
sunflower starfish,
even sparrows,
her green mantle of trees,
letting go of us last?

The Factors That Determine the Outcome of Sperm Competition Are Not Totally Under Male Control. Female Choice Is a Complicating Influence.

p144 of The Insects – An Outline of Entomology fifth edition, P.J. Gullan and P.S. Cranston

hell
yes

What We Know

for Horst

I love you, one of us says.
How do we know? Circumstantial evidence.
Love is hot chocolate, a load of laundry,
going to bed too early with only mild protest.

Love is when you agree to cook
blue cheese pasta without lemon zest.
Hey, we are out of lemons, I say,
and you just shrug, tolerantly.

Love is looking forward all day
to a little me time and after two hours
wondering when you'll come home.
A trash farm on the balcony,

a sock ball in the hall is proof enough!
Love is sharing a beer too small to share.

Aren't We All?

Don't be a baby,
I say to the baby.

Cassandra Watches Netflix

A horror series with a killer baby
helps to calm her down at night,
brief respite from what
she daily sees, the fire,
fire, fire, fire fueled
and fed by ruling men,
while citizens stand doomed,
indifferent and confused.

Bats, They're Just Like Us

April 16 2020, found poem, Wikipedia

In a study on captive Egyptian fruit bats, 60% [of the directed calls]
could be categorized into four contexts: squabbling over food, jostling
over position in their sleeping cluster, protesting over mating attempts
and arguing when perched in close proximity to each other.

Carbon Party

Emissions
are a kind of division
of labor:
some do the easy
jetting, some do
the starving.

At the end
of the universe
everything will decay
into iron,
but before that
is a long time.

A woman flees
her home on fire.
Where can she go?

Hide and Seek

You tell me to hide
and show me where,
so that you're sure
to find me there.

So I Could, So I Did

Having wasted the day,
the wind nibbling,
with small bites of chill,
people walking in coats
of expensive wool,
I nearly didn't go in.
But the sun was still
gilding the trees
on the other shore.
The waves blinked
a last invitation.

Acknowledgements

A big thank you to Jacqueline Saphra, John Glenday, Ruth Wiggins, Shanay Neusum-James, Maggie Dietz, Robert Pinsky, Tim Cresswell, Kirsten Luckins and Vanessa Kisuule for edits and advice in poetry and life.

Big thanks to Amy Acre and Jake Wild Hall for publishing this book and the last, and putting on warm, inclusive and fun events. Thank you to Phil Fried for publishing many of these poems in the *Manhattan Review*.

Thank you to Eunjoo and Russ Thompson, Nawaaz Ahmed and Vic Wu, Carole Allamand, Jyothish George and Purvi Harlalka and especially to Tanay, whose enthusiasm for public transport exceeds even my own. A big schmus for Horst who gets me through the iffy bits and who always brings a magnifying glass.

Anja Konig grew up in the German language and now writes in English. Her first pamphlet *Advice for an Only Child* was shortlisted for the 2015 Michael Marks Prize and her first collection *Animal Experiments* was nominated for the 2021 Laurel Prize. She is madly interested in all living things and can't stop hoping.

Lightning Source UK Ltd.
Milton Keynes UK
UKHW012018171022
410626UK00001B/3